Jack Hull

THE ART OF COMMUNICATING:

Achieving Interpersonal Impact in Business

Bert Decker

D1510906

CRISP PUBLICATIONS, INC.
Los Altos, California

THE ART OF COMMUNICATING

Achieving Interpersonal Impact in Business

Bert Decker

CREDITS
Editor: **Michael G. Crisp**
Designer: **Carol Harris**
Typesetting: **Interface Studio**
Cover Design: **Carol Harris**
Artwork: **Ralph Mapson**

Copyright © 1988 by Decker Communications, Inc.
Printed in the United States of America

English language Crisp books are distributed worldwide. Our major international distributors include:

CANADA: Reid Publishing Ltd., Box 69559—109 Thomas St., Oakville, Ontario Canada L6J 7R4. TEL: (416) 842-4428, FAX: (416) 842-9327

AUSTRALIA: Career Builders, P. O. Box 1051, Springwood, Brisbane, Queensland, Australia 4127. TEL: 841-1061, FAX: 841-1580

NEW ZEALAND: Career Builders, P. O. Box 571, Manurewa, Auckland, New Zealand. TEL: 266-5276, FAX: 266-4152

JAPAN: Phoenix Associates Co., Mizuho Bldg. 2-12-2, Kami Osaki, Shinagawa-Ku, Tokyo 141, Japan. TEL: 3-443-7231, FAX: 3-443-7640

Selected Crisp titles are also available in other languages. Contact International Rights Manager Tim Polk at (415) 949-4888 for more information.

Library of Congress Catalog Card Number 88-73186
Decker, Bert
The Art of Communicating
ISBN 0-931961-45-9

ABOUT THIS BOOK

THE ART OF COMMUNICATING is not like most books. It stands out from other books in an important way. It's not a book to read—it's a book to *use*. The unique "self-paced" format of this book and the many exercises encourage a reader to get involved and try some new ideas immediately.

This book introduces a reader to concepts of interpersonal communication. Using the simple yet sound techniques presented can make a dramatic change in one's ability to achieve excellence while interacting with others.

This book (and the other titles listed in the back of this manual) can be used effectively in a number of ways. Here are some possibilities:

—**Individual Study.** The book is self-instructional. By completing the activities and exercises, a reader should not only receive valuable feedback, but also practical steps for self-improvement.

—**Workshops and Seminars.** The book is ideal for assigned reading prior to a program. With the basics in hand, the quality of participation will improve. The book is also effective when distributed at the beginning of a session, and participants work through the contents.

—**Remote Location Training.** Books can be sent to those not able to attend "home office" training sessions.

There are several other possibilities. One thing for sure, even after it has been read, this book will be looked at—and thought about—again and again.

ABOUT THE AUTHOR

Bert Decker founded the nationally known Decker Communications, Inc. in 1979 to conduct communications training for companies. More than 400 major organizations have enrolled participants in the "Decker Method" during the past two years. Decker is a professional speaker and travels extensively to address large groups in the business community. He has produced and directed over 150 documentary films and commercials (including the Academy Award-winning film "Robert Kennedy Remembered").

THE ART OF COMMUNICATING is based on the "Decker Method" and may be used effectively with a best-selling audiotape program *Speak To Win* and new video release *How To Speak With Confidence,* both produced by Nightingale-Conant Corporation, (800) 323-3938. Decker Communications, Inc. is headquartered at Yerba Buena West, 150 Fourth Street, San Francisco, California 94103, (415) 546-6100.

PREFACE

The communication skills presented in this book can be yours. You will find yourself using them dozens of times a day — both in business and your personal life. They are particularly important to your professional effectiveness because of the increasingly competitive environment. Your personal impact *will* make a difference, and the dozens of ideas presented will assist you.

What we have been taught in school is often not the most effective way to communicate. Listeners are more sophisticated today. *The Art Of Communicating* can provide guidance in learning a wealth of new communication techniques.

Many of the ideas are common sense. Some are new. Most importantly, they all work. They have been tested and proven by over 20,000 business executives, managers and salespeople who have participated in the Decker Method Effective Communicating™ training programs.

Communicating is a skill. It is totally learnable. It takes work, but the results are worth it. With practice you can raise this skill to an art form, and even enjoy the process.

Good luck!

Bert Decker

TABLE OF CONTENTS

SOME IMPORTANT OBJECTIVES FOR THE READER

Achieving excellence in interpersonal communications is a complex process made up of several basic skills. Effective communication is critical to each of us both in work and at play. This book will help you achieve more effective personal communications by introducing you to basic interpersonal skills. It will explain why each is important and allow you to practice the skills presented through a variety of exercises, assessments, check lists and self tests.

After completing this book, I plan to:

☐ Understand the nine basic behavioral skills of effective interpersonal communications.

☐ Practice new techniques that I learn on a daily basis.

☐ Increase my effectiveness in personal communications by working to change one communication habit each day.

☐ Learn to recognize the differences between factual and emotional communications and react accordingly.

☐ Observe the basic signals of behavior to better understand what ''body language'' is really saying.

☐ Encourage practical feedback to insure what is being learned is effectively applied.

THE ART OF COMMUNICATING

Interpersonal communications is not confined to a single aspect of our lives. We communicate interpersonally every time we interact with others. How effectively we do this ultimately determines how successful we become. This book will provide the basics of good interpersonal skills, all of which can be learned and improved upon with practice.

Following is a list of some communication circumstances where interpersonal skills are applied. Read the list and add other situations which require effective interpersonal communication skills. Interpersonal skills are used during:

a job interview.

a business meeting.

a dinner speech.

a candlelight dinner.

a marriage proposal.

a press conference.

a departmental meeting.

a cocktail party.

a stockholder's meeting.

a coffee break.

a play.

a conversation with a friend.

a teacher teaching.

a trainer training.

Add your own:

_____

_____

_____

_____

WHY INTERPERSONAL COMMUNICATION IS AN ART

What It Is

Communicating with another person is not a science. It does not have a regimented set of precise and exacting procedures. There are specific, sound principles and themes, but there are thousands of variations on these themes. Thus it is an *art* to use your skills and capabilities to best advantage within the framework of the principles outlined in this book.

> **Before Renoir, Monet and Cezanne became master artists they first became skilled and expert in basic brush strokes. They learned the principles of painting. Only then were they *free* to create masterpieces.**

This book was designed to give you the "brush strokes" of interpersonal communications so that you too can create a masterpiece during your personal communications with others.

4

THE ART OF COMMUNICATING

A Definition

> As a film producer in the 1970's, Decker Communications was asked to bid on a major documentary motion picture for the National Park Service. Our written proposal helped select us from hundreds of others for a final consideration. Carl, a friend of ours, was on the selection committee. He thought we had a good chance because of our written ideas.
>
> Instead of a formal presentation each finalist had a meeting with the five person committee. Once the meetings were over, our friend had the sad task to inform us we finished third. When we asked for feedback, Carl said, ''You looked nervous. The committee just didn't feel confident about giving your company a half million dollar project.''
>
> It was a tough but important lesson. It demonstrated the importance and power of personal impact in *all* of our communications, formal or informal, large or small, whether to one or one thousand. Having the best idea, strategy or product is simply not enough if it can't be effectively ''sold''. The way in which ideas are sold usually rests with the quality of the presentation skills employed.

Persuasive Communication

The most critical of all personal communication is when we are persuading others. We ''communicate'' our ideas, ourselves or our products to others. At the same time, we are also ''selling'' our ideas, ourselves and our products. *The Art Of Communicating* emphasizes the development of interpersonal skills during persuasive communications.

For example:

- A new business must be able to effectively sell a business plan to obtain financing or credit.

- A supervisor must be able to clearly communicate the goals of the organization to employees.

- A manager must be able to confront an employee who may also be a friend when there is poor performance.

- A parent must be confident enough to speak up at a school board meeting when he or she wants a change.

- An executive, in the midst of a difficult situation, must be calm and confident enough to communicate the facts believably.

Why Apply The Art of Communication

A shy and introspective college sophomore was shocked when his professor said he would never amount to much unless he projected himself more forcefully. This hurt even more because this young man came from a family of leaders. That remark by his professor changed his life because he immediately embarked on an energetic self-improvement program. His name was Norman Vincent Peale.

Some people seem to be born with a natural energy and confidence. Others must work at it. But for all of us, qualities that are most often found in those who lead and succeed *can be learned and strengthened.* All it takes is a conscious effort to learn and apply personal communication skills on a consistent basis with the help of some honest feedback.

Where To Apply Interpersonal Communication Skills

Although the principles, techniques and skills in this book can apply to formal presentations, the emphasis is on the one-on-one communication situations where we daily exert ''personal impact'', (or lack of it.) Some examples of where interpersonal communication skills are required include:

- **Within an Organization:**
  Interviews, meetings, coffee breaks, staff meetings, telephoning, performance reviews, company meetings, hallway conversations, working together on a project, job interviews, lunch breaks, project reviews, negotiating a raise, etc.

- **To Customers or the Public:**
  Customer service, selling, telemarketing, reception desk, association meetings and conventions, TV appearances, telephone press interviews, in-person press interviews, telephoning, promoting, negotiating, etc.

- **In Personal Life:**
  Family meetings, church groups, PTA, parties, telephoning, sports events, pot luck dinners, parent-child discussions, counseling sessions, wedding proposals, etc.

You can apply the principles in this book during most of your waking hours. The opportunities for interpersonal communications are almost limitless.

SECTION I

What Really Counts In Interpersonal Communications

"The ability to express an idea is well nigh as important as the idea itself."

Bernard Baruch

What Really Counts Is Not Usually Taught

The key ingredient to effective communicating is BELIEVABILITY!

Most of us would agree that in business, as in all of life, the believability of the presenter is critical to the success of the presentation. The believability of a person is critical to any interpersonal success. No matter what is said, it is not going to make much difference in the mind of the listener unless a person is credible and believed. There can be no action where there is not belief and agreement.

This is not news to most people. What is news is that *this is not normally taught in our schools.* Even more importantly, *it is not generally the way we conduct our interpersonal communications in business.*

This book reflects the practical application of the latest research, and extensive observation about what really does count during "successful" communications. It applies to "public speaking" as well as the dozens of informal presentations we give daily. Interpersonal communication skill is the ability to continuously build credibility and believability into everything we communicate.

IS EFFECTIVE COMMUNICATION — VERBAL? — VOCAL? — VISUAL?

VERBAL — VOCAL — VISUAL

Professor Albert Mehrabian of UCLA, one of the foremost experts in personal communications, conducted a landmark study on the relationships between the only three elements that are communicated each time we speak.

He measured the difference between the believability of the verbal, vocal and visual elements of our messages. The *verbal* is the message itself—the words that you say. The *vocal* element is your voice—the intonation, projection and resonance of the voice that carries those words. And the *visual* element is what people see— basically what they see of your face and your body. Professor Mehrabian's research found that the degree of inconsistency between these three elements was the factor that determines believability.

In the space provided write your estimate of which element carries the most believability when you are speaking (interpersonal communication) to persuade a listener, and then turn the page to learn the results of Mehrabian's research.

VERBAL	_____	%
VOCAL	_____	%
VISUAL	_____	%
TOTAL	100%	

VERBAL—VOCAL—VISUAL
(Continued)

The Inconsistent Message.

If you give an *inconsistent* message when you are speaking to another person, the following is what Professor Mehrabian found to be the most believable aspects of the three elements in your message discussed on the previous page:

VERBAL	7%
VOCAL	38%
VISUAL	55%
TOTAL	100%

Mehrabian's research (contained in his book, *"Silent Messages"*) was based on what individuals believed when there was an inconsistent message. If the message was consistent, all three elements work together. The excitement and enthusiasm of the voice work with the energy and animation of the face and body to reflect the confidence and conviction of what is said. Here the words, the voice and the delivery are all of a piece and the message gets through.

But in those cases when we are nervous or awkward or under pressure, we tend to block our content and give a very inconsistent message. For example, someone who looks downward, speaks in a halting and tremulous voice, and clasps his or her hands in front in an inhibiting fig leaf position is giving an inconsistent message if that person says, "I am excited to be here". The words will not be believed.

Inconsistency Is the Problem.

Imagine a rocket delivery system. You have the payload, or the rocket ship, which a large Atlas or Titan booster rocket must launch into orbit. If you don't have a strong, powerful rocket, it doesn't matter how well crafted the payload is because it will never get there. The analogy is that our payload is the message that we want to deliver into the heart and mind of our listener. If there is pressure and nervousness, our delivery system will go awry and our payload won't be delivered.

There are few people in business who are like a cannon ready to fire. They are a rocket with no payload. They may have great delivery skills but no mental content. The tragedy is that a large majority of people in business give inconsistent messages. They have detailed, wonderful ideas and productive things to say—technical and financial information—but block the delivery system that is going to get it out there. This inconsistency is probably the biggest barrier to effective interpersonal communications in business.

THE PUBLIC AND PRIVATE SPEAKER

The Public and Private Speaker

We are all public speakers. The only "private speaking" that really goes on is in the privacy of our minds where our ideas bounce back and forth like ping-pong balls. This book refers to the "presentations" we give *daily,* when we present ourselves and our ideas to others. The references here to formal presentations apply as well to the informal ones where people are continuously judging our convictions and abilities.

A PICTURE OF MIKHAIL GORBACHEV

General Secretary Mikhail Gorbachev had an editorial interview with Time Magazine. The writer describing it evokes a picture of what high level personal impact can be when the verbal, vocal and visual elements are consistent. This illustrates interpersonal communications in a formal/informal setting, where Gorbachev conveys the confidence we often strive for.

''He looks well tanned, conveying an image of robust health and naturally controlled energy. He is solid but not fat. He laughs easily.

He dominates a meeting with three extraordinary tools: eyes, hands and voice. The eyes go into action first. They are an intense dark brown. During the conversation they will lock onto a listener and not let go until the listener gives some sign of acknowledgment, agreement—or flinches. The eyes are neither harsh nor kind. They are big and strong.

The hands have a variety of specific functions. The right often holds the steel-rimmed glasses, occasionally manipulating them when Gorbachev pauses to search for a word. The left hand talks. It can lecture, pointing with one finger, or declaim with the palm up, or thump with its edge on the table, karate style, but always quite gently. It is seldom still. Sometimes both hands work together, the fingers clasped, drumming the table for emphasis.

The voice is extraordinary, deep but also quite soft. Sometimes Gorbachev talks for several minutes in a near whisper, low and melodious. Then, without warning, his voice can cut across the room. It is not angry or bullying, just stronger than any other sound in the room. Occasionally the eyes, the hands and the voice reach peak power at the same time, and then it is clear why this man is General Secretary.''

Source: TIME, September 9, 1985

THE PERSONALITY FACTOR

Famed pollster, George Gallup, conducted a poll just two months prior to the U.S. presidential election between Ronald Reagan and Walter Mondale. This poll asked for voters' preference in three areas—issues, party affiliation, and likability or "the personality factor". Here is what Gallup found two months before the general election.

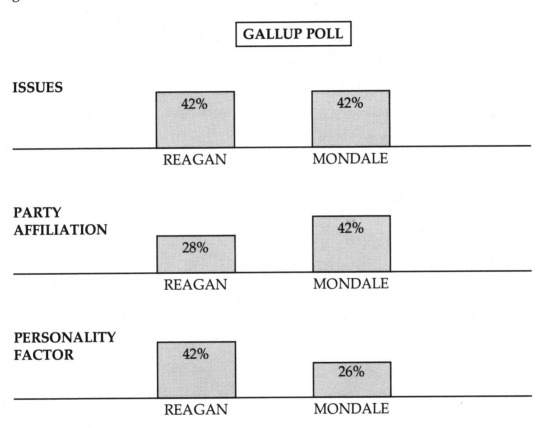

If you added each of these specific preferences on a cumulative basis, you would assume a political race that was "too close to call", if all three factors were equally weighted. But they were not. *The difference in the "personality factor" preference was almost exactly what the difference was in the popular vote two months later—18%.*

This "personality factor", scientifically measured by the Staples Scalometer, has been the only consistent predictor of presidential races in the last eight election campaigns, going back to John F. Kennedy and Richard Nixon.

Like politics, "personality" plays a major role in the effectiveness of an individual's interpersonal relationships. And, despite what you may have read, your personality can be altered and adapted to help improve your interpersonal skills.

THE STANFORD STUDY

Professor Thomas W. Harrell of the Stanford Graduate School of Business*
recently completed a twenty year study relating to career success. While there
were no "certain passports to success", Harrell found there were three consistent
personal qualities that appeared to have a positive affect on the careers of those
studied. These included:

1. An outgoing, ascendant personality
2. A desire to persuade, to talk, and work with people
3. A need for power.

Although interpersonal communication skills are not necessarily related to the
third characteristic, they are certainly intimately intertwined in the first two. This
is the same "personality factor" described on the previous page.

The point is best made with Harrell's conclusion that:

"The consistent variable found which related to management success was the
personality trait of social extroversion or sociability. This variable was consistently
related to success throughout a twenty year career."

---

*Stanford University Study: Harrell & Alpert, March 1986

LEFT BRAIN, RIGHT
BRAIN COMMUNICATIONS

Roger Sperry of the California Institute of Technology won a Nobel prize in his research on the ''two sides of our mind''. His initial findings and subsequent research has a profound effect on understanding interpersonal communications.

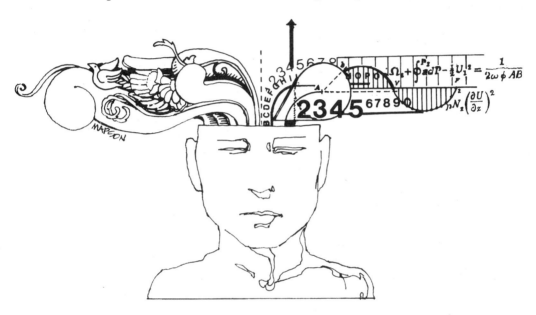

Academic training tends to be oriented to the left side of our brain—multiple choice, and facts and figures. This is the realm of the written medium. Many still teach that it is the realm of the spoken medium as well. However, even though we use words to speak, there is much more involved.

Simply put, if we read a speech, and just tap into the ''left side'' of our listener's mind, we miss reaching the whole brain. We may be speaking in a left brain way, but a listener is listening in right brain mode. She or he is open to all stimuli, and all senses are at work. Our listener can hear, see and smell and has the internal stimuli of mood. The listener may be hungry or full, sleepy, or angry, or peaceful. And you as speaker are communicating hundreds of stimuli in addition to the content.

The right brain is a ''synthesizer''. It is the part of our mind that makes sense of the enormous amounts of stimuli and input which we receive constantly. The right side of the brain is that which deals in parallel processing and pattern recognition. To be effective, in interpersonal relationships, we must speak to the right brain, because our listeners are listening with their right brain dominant.

You will learn how to effectively accomplish this in the next several pages.

SECTION II

Nine Behavioral Skills:
The Key Elements of Interpersonal Communication

It's obvious that vocal delivery and the visual elements, as well as personality, likability and openness are the primary ingredients of high level interpersonal communications. But what specific behavioral characteristics and traits make up these important ingredients?

There are basically nine behavioral skill areas to consider. These are the skills that are emphasized in this book. Each is covered in detail in subsequent pages as shown:

BEHAVIORAL SKILL	PAGE
1. EYE COMMUNICATION	15
2. POSTURE/MOVEMENT	21
3. GESTURES/FACIAL EXPRESSION	27
4. DRESS/APPEARANCE	40
5. VOICE/VOCAL VARIETY	46
6. LANGUAGE/NON-WORDS	53
7. LISTENER INVOLVEMENT	58
8. HUMOR	66
9. THE NATURAL SELF	71

There are literally hundreds of stimuli that go into each behavioral skill area. These are subtle refinements in the perception of the listener. But of these hundreds, there are only a half dozen or so key elements in each of the nine skill areas.

The rest of this book will take you through the nine behavioral skill areas and help you discover skills you already have, and also what skills you need to improve. It will give you practical steps in each area to help you become more effective in all of your interpersonal communications.

BEHAVIORAL SKILL #1: EYE COMMUNICATION

"An eye can threaten like a loaded and leveled gun; or can insult like hissing and kicking; or in its altered mood by beams of kindness, make the heart dance with joy."

Ralph Waldo Emerson

Where and how do you look?

Checklist:

Determine an answer for each question listed below. Repeat this exercise again after you have completed this chapter. You still may need more time **experiencing** your communication relationships to check every box, but review the book on a regular basis until you can complete all of them.

YES NO

☐ ☐ Do you know where you look when you are talking to another person?

☐ ☐ Are you aware where you look when you are listening to another person?

☐ ☐ Do you have a feel for how long to maintain eye communication in a one-on-one conversation?

☐ ☐ Do you know how long to maintain eye communication with specific individuals when presenting to a large group?

☐ ☐ Are you aware where you look when you look away from a person?

☐ ☐ Do you know what eye dart is and whether or not you have it?

☐ ☐ Do you know what "slo-blink" is and why it occurs?

☐ ☐ Do you realize that eye communication is the most important behavioral skill in interpersonal communications?

BEHAVIORAL OBJECTIVE FOR EYE COMMUNICATION

....to look sincerely and steadily at another person.

In individual communications the normal eye communication should be from 5 to 15 seconds. To individuals in a group it should be 4 to 5 seconds. Make this a habit so that when you are under pressure you will maintain a confident eye pattern, without the need to think about it.

WHAT SOME PEOPLE DO

• Doug is minister of a small church. When he leads worship, he keeps his eyes closed 2 to 3 seconds between glances at his audience, causing perhaps a Godly stance, but giving the impression of aloofness. This habit pattern also carries into his personal conversations. He doesn't know he has ''sloblink'', which causes his listeners to feel some distance.

• John is a film producer who habitually looks at the lower right cheek of his listeners. He gives an impression of awkwardness and distance, without knowing it.

• Marion is personnel director for a major corporation. As she interviews people she often looks out her window as she talks and asks questions, appearing uninterested and distant.

• Pat is a great professional speaker, exciting audiences with dramatic personal stories and anecdotes. Except she undermines her personal impact by looking at people in her audience for about half a second, or less. Although she feels she has good eye contact, the individuals in her audience do not feel she is talking right to them.

IMPROVING YOUR EYE COMMUNICATION

Eye communication is the most important skill in your personal impact toolbox. Your eyes are the only part of your central nervous system that directly connect with another person. Don't assume that simply making "eye contact" is enough. Good eye communication means more than just a fleeting glance.

Intimacy, Intimidation and Involvement
The three "I's" of eye communication are intimacy, intimidation and involvement. Intimacy and intimidation mean looking at another person for a long period—from 10 seconds to a minute or more. But over 90% of our personal communications (especially in a business setting) calls for involvement. That deserves our attention and is the basis of the ensuing material.

Five Seconds for More Effectiveness
When we talk to another person and are excited, enthusiastic and confident, we usually look at them for five to ten seconds before looking away. That is what is natural in a one-on-one communication. That's also what you should strive for in all situations—whether speaking to one person or one thousand. This five second period is what listeners are comfortable with in the majority of their communications, so it is logical for you to meet that expectation.

Beware of Eye Dart
The problem most of us have when we feel pressure is to glance at anything but our listener. Our eyes tend to dart every which way like a scared rabbit. This conveys a nervousness that undermines our credibility. Anything other than looking directly at the person we are talking to increases this tendency and makes our listener uncomfortable.

Beware of Slo-Blink
On the other hand, it is equally disconcerting to develop a habit of "slo-blink". This is where you might keep your eyelids closed for up to 2 or 3 seconds. It conveys the message, "I really don't want to be here." Usually, your listeners won't want to either.

Eye Communication and Television
With the advent of the video age, we all will be on TV (as a training vehicle or perhaps home videotape) sooner or later. It is important to have good steady eye communication with the interviewer and any others that the camera can see. Never look directly at the camera. The TV audience is really observing you through the means of the camera, so treat the camera as the "observer" it really is.

IMPROVING YOUR
EYE COMMUNICATION
(Continued)

Angle of Eye Incidence

One final tip. If you are addressing a large group and your angle of eye incidence between each individual is small, extended eye communication (5 seconds) is even more important. This is because when you look at one person, dozens of people around that person will think you are talking just to them.

Application to Business

You use your eyes to communicate 90% of the time in business (excluding the telephone.) As you communicate to people you encounter in business (colleagues, customers, superiors, etc.), concentrate on how you look at them. Envision how you look when you are upset or are pleased. As a salesperson focus on how you look at tough clients prior to a sale. Compare that to how you look when you have just closed a sale. Notice the eye patterns of others during job interviews and performance appraisals. Then take that new found awareness and apply it to more effective and confident eye patterns of your own.

Following are several skill development exercises and tips to extend your eye communications in those dozens of interpersonal communications you have daily. Practice each of them on a daily basis. At first things may feel awkward or embarassing, but like other learned behaviors, regular practice will increase your confidence and your ''eye communication'' will show steady improvement.

EXERCISES IN EYE COMMUNICATION AWARENESS AND SKILL DEVELOPMENT

1. *Where do you look?* In your next ten conversations, determine where you generally look when you talk to others. Note that you *do not* look directly in both eyes. You may look at either a person's left eye or right eye, but it is impossible to look at both at the same time. In one-to-one conversations, eyes tend to move around a face, but there is one predominant place most of us tend to rest. Find where your spot is—the right eye? bridge of nose? left eye? or directly between the eyes? Any resting place near the eyes is acceptable. Not acceptable is anywhere else (i.e. the floor, over your listener's shoulder, etc.).

Once you have found your pattern, increase your awareness and sensitize yourself to the complexities of eye communication. Then try to look somewhere else, and feel the dissonance. This will help desensitize you to the feelings of awkwardness when you might not want to look directly at someone, but should for effectiveness.

2. *Reinforce the five second habit.* When you are in a meeting or giving a speech, ask a friend to count how long you look at specific individuals. Consciously keep five second eye communication with individuals in the group to whom you are communicating.

3. *Increase Sensitivity.* Talk to a partner for about a minute. Ask the partner to look away from you after 15 seconds as you continue talking. For the rest of the exercise have your partner look anywhere else but at you while he or she is still listening. How does this feel? Reverse this process, and then discuss the relevance of eye communication in verbal conversations. Notice how often good eye contact is lacking at certain social functions (i.e. parties). Practice better eye contact in these informal situations and notice what a difference it makes to a conversation.

4. *Relieve intimidation.* If you feel uncomfortable with an individual that you must talk to (such as in a job interview or a meeting with the President of the company), try looking at that person's forehead. To experiment with this, get in a conversation with a partner sitting 4 or 5 feet away. Look at the middle of his or her forehead, just above the eyes. That person will think you have good eye communication with them. But you will not feel like you are "in touch" at all. This will help reduce the emotional connection so it is almost as if you are talking to a wall. Reverse the process so your partner can experience the same phenomenon.

5. *Tips.* Observe others (either in person or on TV) and notice how different an individual's eye communication patterns make you feel about them. Videotape yourself so you can see your eye patterns. Ask friends how they feel about your eye communication. Ask a friend or associate to analyze your eye contact in various communication circumstances.

PERSONAL GOAL WORKSHEET

Habits to Evaluate:

Write down three of your habitual patterns regarding your eye communication that you may want to modify, strengthen or lose:

1.

2.

3.

Then write what you plan to practice to modify, strengthen or change each habit.

1.

2.

3.

Remember: Practice Makes Permanent

BEHAVIORAL SKILL #2: POSTURE AND MOVEMENT

''Stand tall. The difference between towering and cowering is totally a matter of inner posture. It's got nothing to do with height, it costs nothing and it's more fun.''

Malcolm Forbes

How do you hold yourself?

Checklist:

Determine an answer for each question listed below. Repeat this exercise again after you have completed this chapter. You still may need more time **experiencing** your communication relationships to check every box, but review the book on a regular basis until you can complete all of them.

YES NO

☐ ☐   Do you lean back on one hip when you are talking in a small group?

☐ ☐   Do you cross your legs when you are standing and chatting informally?

☐ ☐   Is your upper body posture erect? Are your shoulders in a straight line or do they curve inwards towards your chest?

☐ ☐   When you speak formally, do you plant yourself behind a lectern or table?

☐ ☐   Do you communicate impatience by tapping your foot or a pencil when you are listening?

☐ ☐   Do you know if you have the ''fig leaf'' or other nervous or inhibiting gesture habits when addressing a group?

☐ ☐   Do you move around when talking informally?

BEHAVIORAL OBJECTIVE

. . . .to learn to stand tall and move naturally and easily.

You must be able to correct the general tendency to "slump" in both upper and lower body posture. When communicating it is more effective to be fluid rather than locked into rigid positions. This applies to gestures, but particularly leg and foot movements.

WHAT SOME PEOPLE DO

• Phyllis runs her own consulting firm. She thought she had a big tummy as a little girl, so she consciously sucked in her stomach at all times. This caused her shoulders to go back, so that as an adult she has very erect body posture. Because of the confident way she walks, she commands attention when she enters a room.

• Eric works in a television studio. He grew so fast that in eighth grade he was 6'2". He tried to diminish his height by slumping. Now, as an adult, he is a stoop shouldered 6'6". Although he has the self esteem he lacked as a youngster, his early posture habit causes him to appear hesitant and lacking in confidence.

• Al is president of a major transportation company. He attended an executive seminar with several of his employees. Because of his poor posture, the seminar leader first perceived him as an employee rather than the boss.

• Denise was 17 when she volunteered to participate in a videotape demonstration during a communications seminar. She was to talk for a few minutes, then the during the next week participate in the seminar before returning to talk on camera again. She was participating in a "before & after" experiment. Although several things were different, most remarkable was her posture change. When she first talked she leaned on her left hip, and was casually stooped. The next week the TV audience first saw her as she strode from behind the curtain and stood tall. Even before she opened her mouth, she exuded a confidence that was almost tangible.

IMPROVING YOUR POSTURE & MOVEMENT

Think of a public figure you often see on TV. Can you think of any who are "slumpers"? Probably not many, since confidence is usually expressed through excellent posture.

How you hold yourself physically can reflect how you hold yourself mentally. And how you hold yourself is usually how others regard you. People tend to treat you exactly as you ask to be treated.

► *Stand Tall*

Poor upper body posture often reflects low self-esteem. Not always, but other people always see it that way until they have enough other information to change this opinion. Many times upper body posture comes from an outdated habit pattern. Many tall men walk around hunched over because they grew fast as teenagers and didn't want to stand out. Others simply never considered posture to be important and allowed the slouching and slumping "teenage" period to extend into adulthood.

► *Watch Your Lower Body*

The second part of posture that often gets neglected is the lower body. When you are talking to others you may decrease your effectiveness because of the way you stand. You can divert your communication energy away from your listeners through inappropriate body language. One of the most common adverse posture patterns is "going back on one hip." If you tend to go back on one hip you are subconsciously saying "I don't want to be here," and literally distance yourself from others. Other variations are rocking from side to side, going back and forth on your heels and toes, or pacing.

► *Use the "Ready Position"*

What you can do to combat these negative habits is to take the "ready position." The ready position means basically weight forward. Communication rides on a horse of "energy". When you are speaking—when you are confident and want to get your message across—you have your energy forward. The "ready position" is leaning slightly forward so you could bounce up and down on the balls of your feet, with your knees slightly flexed. It is similar to practicing for competition in athletics where you are ready to move in any direction. When your weight is forward, it is impossible to go back on one hip or rock back and forth on your heels. Get in the habit of the "ready position" in both formal and informal communication situations, and you'll be **ready** when the heat is on.

IMPROVING YOUR POSTURE & MOVEMENT
(Continued)

► *Move*

Communication and energy cannot be separated. Use all of your natural energy in a positive fashion. When you are speaking to others, move around. Come out from behind the lectern if you are in a formal situation. This will remove the physical barrier between yourself and others. In a group meeting, you have space to move a bit—your feet as well as your hands or arms. In a seated situation you might think of standing when you are ''on'', or leaning forward to give yourself more impact. Movement adds to your energy, reflects confidence and adds variety to your communications. Don't overdo it, but do move within your own natural energy level. Although high energy people have an advantage, greater personal impact is available to all who stay conscious of using what they have.

► *Your Own Style*

Be sure to adapt posture and movement concepts to your personal style. There is no absolute right or wrong way to stand or move. But there are concepts that work. Two of these are ''stand erect'' and ''keep your energy forward'' when you are communicating. Think of them as your ''ready position'' and then work to fit them to your personal style.

EXERCISES IN AWARENESS AND SKILL DEVELOPMENT

1. *See Yourself.* Posture and movement is one skill set that you can readily observe. Mirrors or through the assistance of observation of others will help. Better yet, if you can arrange it, observe yourself walking and talking on videotape. Notice what your upper body communicates—standing tall? hunching down? somewhere in between? If you cross your legs and lean against walls when you are standing informally, you will notice that it often appears sloppy rather than casual. Try variations of the "ready position" to see how that looks.

2. *Walk Away From The Wall.* The upper body posture of beauty pageant contestants is erect and confident. One reason is the "walk away from the wall" exercise learned from Miss America, Donna Axum. She suggests standing against a wall with your heels and shoulders touching the wall. Then straighten your spine so that the small of your back is also touching the wall. Walk away from the wall, (shake a little so you are not rigid), and then walk a few steps. Notice how you **feel** tall, and project more confidence. If you practice this regularly you can improve your posture dramatically.

3. *Do The "Two-step".* The next time you are talking to a group, have someone count the number of steps you take, (if you move at all). Then think of the "two-step." Often we take tentative half-steps because we want to move, but feel inhibited. That degree of movement is better than none, but still reflects exactly what we feel— tentativeness. If you do the "two-step", taking at least two steps **towards** someone, you will force yourself to move with apparent purpose. When you combine that with good eye communication, you will be talking and presenting yourself in a confident, direct fashion.

4. *Stand At Meetings.* Experiment with posture and movement. At your next meeting, stand when you have something important to say. This will give your message more emphasis. When you go into a one-on-one meeting to sell a product or an idea, consider making a stand-up presentation, perhaps even using a visual device such as a "flip chart". You can have fun trying new ways to use your posture and movement for maximum effect, and gain some impact in the process.

PERSONAL GOAL WORKSHEET

Habits to Evaluate:

Write down three of your habitual patterns regarding posture and movement that you may want to modify, strengthen or lose:

1.

2.

3.

Then write what you plan to practice to modify, strengthen or change each habit.

1.

2.

3.

Remember: Practice Makes Permanent

BEHAVIORAL SKILL #3: GESTURES/FACIAL EXPRESSIONS

"We don't 'know' our presidents. We imagine them. We watch them intermittently and from afar, inferring from only a relatively few gestures and reactions what kind of people they are and whether they should be in charge. Much depends on our intuition and their ability at a handful of opportune moments to project qualities we admire and respect."

Meg Greenfield

Are you aware how you look to others?

Checklist:

Determine an answer for each question listed below. Repeat this exercise again after you have completed this chapter. You still may need more time **experiencing** your communication relationships to check every box, but review the book on a regular basis until you can complete all of them.

YES NO

☐ ☐ Do you smile under pressure, or does your face become a stone face?

☐ ☐ When you talk on the phone, do you find yourself smiling or frowning?

☐ ☐ Do you have an inhibiting gesture—an awkward place where your hands tend to go when speaking under pressure?

☐ ☐ Do you ever raise your hand or arm above waist level when making a presentation to a group?

☐ ☐ Do you lean forward and gesture when you are seated, just as you do when you are making a presentation?

☐ ☐ Do you communicate impatience by drumming your fingers on the table when you are listening?

☐ ☐ Do your fingers twitch if you try to keep them at your sides when you are speaking to a group?

BEHAVIORAL OBJECTIVE

....to learn to be relaxed and natural when you speak

To be effective at interpersonal communication you should have your hands and your arms relaxed and natural at your sides when you are at rest. You should gesture naturally when animated and enthusiastic. You should learn to smile under pressure, in the same way you would with a natural smile when you are comfortable.

WHAT SOME PEOPLE DO

• Former U.S. President Jimmy Carter was considered to have unusually low energy. Carter's media advisor inadvisably suggested that he show more energy by gesturing during a televised speech. Ironically, the topic of the speech was the "Energy Crisis". President Carter's teleprompter was marked at certain key words for him to emphasize with gestures. It looked so awkward and uncomfortable that it was written up the next day by reporters. The stories said Carter looked like a "wooden puppet". The moral is that everyone, (even presidents), should work within their natural energy framework.

• Ted participated in a video tape seminar where he gave a two minute introduction. He started with a nervous gesture called the "fig leaf", but he quickly switched into something much worse. He began raising his cupped hands every two seconds. When he saw it later on video playback, he called himself the "fig leaf flasher". He was so shocked at the distraction that he worked to change his habit and never "flashed" again.

• Charles rose through the ranks to become senior vice president of a major advertising agency. His employees thought he was always in a bad mood because his face looked grim and serious. He was also quizzical when his children would say, "What's wrong, Dad?" It wasn't until he did some experimenting in front of a video camera that he saw what others meant. Even when smiling on the inside, nothing showed through on the outside. Surprisingly, when he tried to exaggerate a smile, it didn't look exaggerated—but showed excitement and enthusiasm.

IMPROVING YOUR GESTURES AND FACIAL EXPRESSIONS

What Works

Communication reflects energy. Those born with extra energy have an advantage. However, we all can be aware of and increase our energy levels. These are most apparent in our gestures and facial expressions.

To communicate effectively, you need to be as open as possible in your face and gestures—*as it is natural for you to do.* You can work to insure better gestures and facial expressions in the following ways:

► *Find Out Your Habits*
Find how you look to others when you are under pressure. Get this to the conscious level. You can make this discovery through feedback from others, but best of all, view and observe yourself on video tape. You have to know what you are doing that is *not natural* before you can be *natural.* You need to be able to recognize your habits at a level of "conscious incompetence". (See the next section on Habits.)

► *Find Your Nervous Gestures*
We all have "nervous gestures", a place we tend to go with our hands when we are speaking and don't have any thing to hold onto. Find out what your primary gesture is, and then *do anything but* that gesture. Don't try to gesture at certain words or phrases—it doesn't work well. Just concentrate on not doing your nervous gesture. Ultimately your hands should fall to your sides when you are not emphasizing an idea or point. When you do want the emphasis that comes from natural enthusiasm, it will occur naturally. But it can't occur if your hands are continually locked in a nervous gesture like the fig leaf or the arm lock (see illustration on page 28).

► *You Can't Over-Exaggerate*
Suprisingly very, very few people exaggerate their gestures or facial expressions. This is such a dramatic finding, that it is almost possible to say that you cannot over-exaggerate. Push yourself. Try to exaggerate your positive gestures. You'd be surprised about how normal they actually look. Don't worry about overdoing it.

► *Smile—Which Third Are You In*
We *all* think that we smile much of the time. In reality, others observe us as having a very strong predisposition to either smiling or not smiling. Studies have shown that approximately one-third of people in business have naturally open and smiling faces. The middle third tend to have neutral faces which can readily go from a smile to a serious and intense look. The "lower third" have faces that are serious and intense, whether they think they are smiling or not.

IMPROVING YOUR GESTURES AND FACIAL EXPRESSIONS (Continued)

▶ *Smile—Which Third Are You In? (Continued)*
Find out which third you are in. Ask others to help you. If you are in the easily smiling third, you have a distinct advantage in your communications with others. People will perceive you as open and friendly, and will be more open to your ideas. Another advantage is that you can also convey bad news more readily than others. If you are in the neutral third, easily moving from a smiling face to a serious one, you have flexibility. But if you are in the lower one-third you have to work on this area of your communications. You may be smiling on the inside, but your face may reflect doom and gloom on the outside. That is exactly what you communicate. Perception is reality in the eyes of the beholder.

▶ *Remember the "Personality Factor"*
Your gestures, particularly your facial expression, will tend to show you to be open and close, or closed and distant to those with whom you are communicating. "He who would have friends, let him show himself friendly." (Proverbs 18:24) Remember that people will buy your ideas and be persuaded much more readily if they like you. People like those who are more open. It pays to cultivate the "personality factor". Serious people, such as technocrats, analysts, programmers, engineers, academicians, etc., can be effective in person. But they are usually more effective in writing. Interpersonal communications means connecting with another person on an emotional level, not just an intellectual level.

▶ *Smiles Have Muscles*
There's nothing mysterious about a smile, except the effect it has. It is physically caused by muscles and they can be exercised. The best way to practice smiling is not by moving your lips into a smile as much as it is raising your cheek bones. Consider the upper part of your cheeks as apples and just lift your apples to smile. Put muscle in your smile.

▶ *Caution: Phony Smiles Don't Work*
We emphasize the importance of smiling in your interpersonal efforts because that immediately communicates how people perceive you are feeling. They look at your face and the smile dominates the face. So it is important to become aware of how you smile and to practice and exercise the "smile muscle". But, be aware that phony smiles don't work. Not only do they not last—they are perceived as phony. You want to train the skill through practice with your facial muscles, but remember that a true smile comes from within. It is like an athlete who practices and trains his or her muscles so that they are ready to use at the right time, motivated by the adrenalin of the real situation.

EXERCISES IN AWARENESS AND SKILL DEVELOPMENT

1. PLAY WITH A PARTNER.

Stand six to eight feet from another person who will be your observer. Talk about how your hands and arms feel as they are resting at your sides. Then continue talking about gestures in general and how they feel when they are natural, gesturing as you do so. Then exaggerate your gestures, even moving a little bit if you feel like it, and describe to your partner how awkward and foolish you might be feeling. Make sure your gestures *are* exaggerated—and that they definitely go above your waist and out to the side. Then ask your partner for feedback. You probably will be surprised that your partner does not feel that you over-exaggerated as much as you felt you did. Reverse the process and let your partner do the gesturing and you give the feedback. Practice at this exercise several times until you get a good feel of how "energetic" you can actually be without being perceived as exaggerated.

2. COUNT YOUR NERVOUS GESTURES.

The next time you speak in front of a group, have someone count the number of times you display your nervous gesture. This can be at a meeting or in a formal or informal speaking situation. If you have the fig leaf, for example, tell your observer that your nervous gesture is the fig leaf, and then have that person count the number of times that you actually you do the fig leaf during the presentation. This will sensitize you to how serious your problem is, and will also be a good way to start your program of behavior modification *to do anything but* your distracting gesture.

3. ROLE PLAYING.

Look at a video tape or TV performance of a confident, forceful and energetic speaker, and practice emulating him or her. Pick a natural leader from politics, business or athletics. Remember that this is just a role play and practice, so put all of yourself in it:

• Take an actual presentation, preferably a business presentation, and deliver it to another person or group of people as you normally would. (This exercise is very effective in groups.)

• Then think about how your "role model" might deliver it.

• Put all of yourself into "acting as if" you are that person delivering your material. Let it all hang out.

• Then ask for feedback from the group. (If possible videotape both the "before and after" and you will then be able to *see* the difference in yourself.)

EXERCISES IN AWARENESS AND SKILL DEVELOPMENT
(Continued)

You will normally find that your second presentation had more conviction and believability than your first. Remember that this is only an exercise, and should not imply that you need to act like somebody else in real life. But it should make you aware of how much more energy you have available if you choose to use it, adapting to your own style.

4. GO TO A DEPARTMENT STORE.
Video tape feedback is extremely valuable for all of the behavioral skill areas talked about in this book, but particularly so for gestures and facial expression. Find a way to get yourself on video tape. If you have no other access, here is a way that can work for everybody. Go to your local department store and ask them to demonstrate a video camera. Have them tape you doing a minute or so of an impromptu little talk and ask them to replay it. The following week go to another store and do the same thing. After several times, you will have experienced the invaluable process of video feedback. Then decide which system is best for you and if you can afford a camera, buy one.

5. WATCH TELEVISION WITH NO SOUND.
One day look at television—from situation comedies to talk shows to the news—but turn the sound off. If you do that just five or ten minutes a day you will be amazed at how much is communicated by those you observe. Their interpersonal communications, believability, confidence and credibility as individuals is largely conveyed through their gestures and facial expression.

6. TEST YOUR SMILE.
This exercise can be done by yourself if you have access to a video camera. Start the tape, look directly at the camera and give a big phony smile. Describe to the camera how it feels to give that big phony smile. Spend twenty or thirty seconds with that big phony smile. Then, with the video tape continuing to run, wipe your face clean and convey what to you feels like a normal, easy, friendly smile. Describe how that feels on your face for twenty to thirty seconds. Then view your video tape. If you are one of the bottom third of ''nonsmilers'', you will probably be surprised that your phony smile doesn't look as bad as you thought, and at least conveys some degree of openness and friendliness. At the same time the natural smile you felt on the inside does not show at all on the outside. In many cases when you think you are smiling, you're actually looking serious.

PERSONAL GOAL WORKSHEET

Habits to Evaluate:

Write down three of your habitual patterns regarding your use of gestures/facial expressions that you may want to modify, strengthen or lose:

1.

2.

3.

Then write what you plan to practice to modify, strengthen or change each habit.

1.

2.

3.

Remember: Practice Makes Permanent

INTERLUDE:

HABITS

Although all behaviors come from our habits, it is essential at this stage to talk about habit formation. How habits are formed and how to change them.

Maxwell Maltz, in his book, ''Psycho-Cybernetics'', said that it takes twenty-one days to change a habit. Other studies have verified this. There are hundreds of interpersonal communication habits all of us have, both positive and negative. Most are within the basic nine communication skill areas covered in this book. To change any habit takes practice—framing, forming, and molding our minds to do certain physical behaviors that are repeated over and over again.

The problem is that habits can seem like a huge elephant on our backs:

The only way to cut that elephant down to size is to wittle it down to bite-size pieces. It's the same with our habits. To change them takes practice in bite size pieces.

CHANGING HABITS

Think about the following habits you have. Those described below are harmless but ingrained:

1. Fold your arms. Now do it the opposite way. Notice that when you fold your arms you automatically had one way to do it. When you tried the opposite way it seemed strange and uncomfortable.

2. Clasp your hands together, putting one thumb over the other. Now reverse the process. You will find that one way was more comfortable for you. (By the way this is seldom related to left-handedness or right-handedness, as to which thumb over feels more comfortable.)

3. Do you always brush your teeth in the morning, or at night? Do you have the same order when you wash your hands, your face, or take a shower?

4. Do you always take the same route or transportation to work, or do you vary these things?

5. Think of your eating habits: whether you have milk, water, or wine with a meal; whether you eat your vegetables, meat, or potatoes first; whether you eat fast or slowly; what you eat; what restaurants you go to regularly; and when you go to the same restaurant whether you eat the same things, etc.

All of these habits are not necessarily good or bad, but they are habits. And because they are habits, *you seem to have no choice about how you do them at the conscious level.* Since it is not particularly important whether you fold your arms or hands a certain way or eat a certain food first, it doesn't make much sense to change these habits. But there are habits that are worth working on. In interpersonal communications, some habits will either enhance or detract from your effectiveness. That is what we want to concentrate on. But be aware that, as creatures of habit, we are not easily changed, so don't give up if things don't change overnight.

EXERCISE

Throughout this book we suggest specific communication habits to change. To sensitize yourself and increase your habit changing skills, following are some ideas:

Change three habits. Make it a campaign to work on them every day, day in and day out.

1. These habits should be simple, little, everyday habits you may want to change (i.e. to read for pleasure, at least fifteen minutes each day.)

2. It is most effective to *jar* your habit formation. Take one morning habit, one afternoon habit and one evening habit for starters.

3. Look at the different areas of your life for your "habit changes", i.e., eating habits, sleeping habits, coffee break habits, recreation habits, sexual habits, dressing habits, work habits,etc.

In the next few pages we will cover Abraham Maslow's "Four Steps of Learning" and learn how they are related to the "Four Stages of Speaking." This information should allow you to evaluate and prioritize which of your interpersonal habits need work—and give you some practical guidelines about how to make positive improvements in your interpersonal effectiveness.

THE FOUR STAGES OF LEARNING

Abraham Maslow has given us a valuable conceptual framework to understand how we learn *anything:*

1. *Unconscious Incompetence*

We don't know that we don't know.

An energetic two year old boy wants to ride a bike that he sees his older brother riding. But he doesn't know that he doesn't know how to ride it. All he says is, ''Mommy, I want to ride the bike.'' Most of us in business who have never had extensive feedback about our interpersonal skills are at this state of unconscious incompetence. We simply are not aware of our interpersonal communication habits.

2. *Conscious Incompetence*

We know that we don't know.

Here we learn that we are not competent at something. This often comes as a rude awakening. The two year old boy gets on a bike and falls off. He has immediately gone from stage one to stage two and knows that he does not know how to ride a bike. Just as a communicator with ''slow blink'' or ''the fig leaf'' knows for the first time that he or she has a distracting eye pattern or gesture when it is realized first hand by that person.

3. *Conscious Competence*

We work at what we don't know.

Here we consciously make an effort to learn a new skill. Practice, drill and repetition are at the forefront. This is where most learning takes place. It takes effort and work. The little boy carefully steers and balances and pedals and thinks of what he is doing, step by step. The person with slow blink (or a fig leaf or non-words or monotone, etc.) consciously works at changing a distracting habit.

4. *Unconscious Competence*

We don't have to think about knowing it.

Here the skill set happens automatically at an unconscious level. The little boy rides his bike without even thinking about it. He can whistle, talk, sing, or do other things with his mind at the same time. A speaker with a distracting habit who has learned to overcome it through practice doesn't have to concentrate on *not* doing the distracting habit.

THE FOUR STAGES OF SPEAKING

The four stages of speaking are related to the four stages of learning, although they are not parallel. All communicators are in one of the four stages of speaking. To advance from one to another requires going through the four stages of learning.

Stage 1. The Non Speaker

People at this level avoid "public" speaking at all costs. The emotional set is one of terror. They will go to great lengths not to speak formally. They sometimes get trapped, but in general are adept at finding excuses (like illness) so they won't have to present themselves or their ideas publicly. Their interpersonal communication skills tend to be low, and they generally work in jobs that do not require speaking skills.

Stage 2. The Occasional Speaker

People at this level reluctantly accept speaking assignments. They almost never volunteer. However, they recognize that they must be able to present their ideas if they want to get ahead. They will speak when necessary. Their fear is inhibiting, but not debilitating. This is the easiest stage to advance from—just by practicing the act of speaking.

Stage 3. The Willing Speaker

Fear is not a drawback at this level. The emotional set here is one of tension. This speaker has learned to use emotions positively. They will speak their minds in business meetings. In general they are willing to put themselves out front— although they sometimes need a little nudge—and they know they will do well. But they still have some trepidation.

Stage 4. The Leader

Speaking stimulates these folks. They are driven to present themselves and their ideas—they know the rewards to be reaped. The Leaders literally "speak for a living" by motivating their people and speaking up and out in all situations. They can inspire, and their roles in business are, by definition, as leaders.

HOW VIDEO FEEDBACK CAN CHANGE SPEAKING HABITS

The San Francisco State Study*

As can be seen from the four learning stages, awareness of habits is critical to any behavior change. Change comes most readily from feedback. In the case of interpersonal communications, video feedback is especially effective.

Our interpersonal communications effectiveness is directly related to our confidence. It is valuable, therefore, to know how to create changes from video feedback. People are better than they think they are, once they become objectively aware about how they come across to others.

San Francisco State University sponsored a study that documents such changes. A statistically valid survey was done with 2,000 participants who participated in an intensive 2-day video feedback program. They placed themselves in four stages of speaking *before* having video feedback and then again *after* seeing themselves in different communicating circumstances during the 2-day period.

Following are the results:

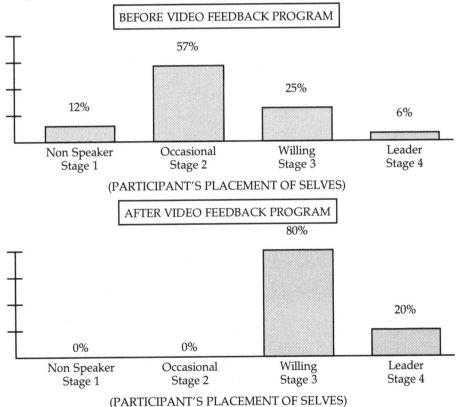

BEFORE VIDEO FEEDBACK PROGRAM

57%

25%

12%

6%

Non Speaker
Stage 1

Occasional
Stage 2

Willing
Stage 3

Leader
Stage 4

(PARTICIPANT'S PLACEMENT OF SELVES)

AFTER VIDEO FEEDBACK PROGRAM

80%

20%

0%

0%

Non Speaker
Stage 1

Occasional
Stage 2

Willing
Stage 3

Leader
Stage 4

(PARTICIPANT'S PLACEMENT OF SELVES)

* S.F. State Business School Study, 1985

The Art of Communicating: Achieving Interpersonal Impact in Business

BEHAVIORAL SKILL #4: DRESS AND APPEARANCE

"You never get a second chance to make a *good*, first impression."

John Molloy

DO YOU DRESS FOR WORK BY HABIT, OR BY DESIGN?

Checklist:

Determine an answer for each question listed below. Repeat this exercise again after you have completed this chapter. You still may need more time **experiencing** your communication relationships to check every box, but review the book on a regular basis until you can complete all of them.

YES   NO

☐   ☐   Do you look better with your hair parted where it is now, or parted on the other side, or frizzed, permed, crew-cut, sprayed or tinted?

☐   ☐   Do your glasses inhibit good eye communication?

☐   ☐   Do you look different with glasses or contact lenses? Is there a difference in effectiveness?

☐   ☐   Are clothes in your closet organized out of habit, or by design?

☐   ☐   Do people notice your jewelry?

☐   ☐   Are people distracted by your jewelry?

☐   ☐   Do you ever dress to shock people, or for effect, or for any reason other than to cover your body?

☐   ☐   Are you always aware of your grooming? (Are your nails trimmed and clean? Do you bathe daily? Are your clothes always clean and pressed? etc.)

BEHAVIORAL OBJECTIVE

....to dress, groom, and appear appropriate to the environment that you are in, as well as to yourself.

Some Personal Examples

• For almost 15 years the author of this book had a beard. The response I received was mostly positive, and I liked it. When it began to turn grey, I thought of tinting it, but decided to shave it off. After a few days I learned that 90% of the people I talked to liked the beardless Bert better. ''Look 5 to 10 years younger,'' I often heard, and was struck at the difference it made in others' perception of me.

• Also, as a film producer several years ago, I used to go around in the tieless ''uniform'' of the filmaker. When speaking to business groups it was a concession to wear a tie and jacket. Today I am embarassed to think of the audiences' reaction the time I spoke to the 50 managers of a client company with a plaid sports jacket and black knit tie standing out from a background of a vivid red shirt.

IMPROVING YOUR DRESS AND APPEARANCE

We form immediate and vivid impressions of people during the first five seconds we see them. Experts estimate that it takes another five minutes to add fifty percent more impression, (negative or positive), to the impression we made in the first five seconds. (We are talking about emotional impression rather than content, or intellectual impression.)

Since ninety percent of our persona is covered by clothing, we need to be aware of what our clothes are communicating. (By the way, when we are uncovered, the same principle applies. Considering this, if we spend time at the beach, we might be motivated to exercise a bit more often.)

The ten percent of our body not normally covered by clothes is largely our face and hair. This is the most important ten percent of all because this is where people look. The impression others receive is very much influenced by the style of how we groom our head, (i.e., hairstyle, make-up and jewelry for women, hairstyle, facial hair or lack of it for men, etc.).

Be Appropriate

The most important two words for effective dress are "**be appropriate**." There is not so much a right or wrong way to dress or groom, as an appropriate way. This means appropriate first of all as to how comfortable *you* feel. This is more important than what others feel. If you feel uncomfortable, you will not communicate very effectively. Your appearance should be appropriate to the company you are in, (the expectations of others, your geographical setting, the time of day, social situation, circumstances, etc.).

Dress At The Conscious Level

Since we are creatures of habits, most of us dress based on past habits. Take a careful and conscious look at how you dress and groom. Do you pick out a certain color because you always have? Does that color work for you? Do you wear certain ties or bows because that's what you did in college? Is it effective today?

It's Bigger Than You Think

The effect of your initial appearance on others is far greater than you think. It is not a superficial thing, but communicates extensively to others how you feel about yourself. It also shows what you sometimes do just to get attention.

EXERCISES IN AWARENESS AND SKILL DEVELOPMENT

1. **The First Five Seconds.**
   When you next meet a person for the first time, consciously keep a mental picture of how you *felt* about that person after the first impresssion. Then analyze how much came from dress, from expression, from how the hair was styled, from eye contact, jewelry, etc. What made a positive impression and what made a distracting impression? What was neutral? Do this exercise daily. It can also be an enjoyable pastime at a party or social gathering.

2. **Pick Five People.**
   Write the names of five people you know well. Think of how you would *design* their dress and appearance differently. Pick it apart in detail—the clothes, shirts, skirts, ties, colors, patterns, make-up, hair, jewelry, glasses, etc. It works best if you write out the changes so you will become *consciously* aware of the differences each of these elements make.

3. **Nobody Will Tell You.**
   Now that you have analyzed five other people, do the same for yourself. Analyze in detail what you do and what you should change. Realize that almost nobody will volunteer to tell you. What needs changing? Dress and appearance is one of the most self-conscious and personally sensitive issues in interpersonal communications, so few people will tell us what they really think and feel. You can help them provide feedback by just asking. It can help verify your own analysis.

4. **Pick A New Outfit.**
   Every day look at something in a new way. Choose one area, like your shoes, dress, suit, jacket, tie, shirt, and/or grooming and appearance habit. Change it. Combine it with something to give a new look. Pick an appropriate but different outfit the next time you are shopping. Dressing differently daily will sensitize you to how *you* feel in your dress and appearance, and will also make you more aware of how others feel about your appearance. You will also discover what works well.

EXERCISES IN AWARENESS AND SKILL DEVELOPMENT (Continued)

5. **See A Consultant**

   Since dress and appearance have a great impact on how others perceive us, it is often worth the time and expense to consult with a specialist. This can be a clothes consultant, color consultant or make-up consultant. Be sure to check referrals as this is an area of ''image intangibles'' and you want to be sure you get good advice. You can consult specialized ''buyers'' in retail department stores to assist in your clothes buying.

6. **Research, Research, Research.**

   Read a book. John Molloy's books are probably the best known, (''How To Dress For Success'' in both men's and women's versions) Although his opinions may not be your cup of tea, his research is extensive and the ''rights and wrongs'' according to Molloy are valuable to know. Also read magazine and newspaper articles on the subject. Although they too are filled with subjective opinions, they will help increase your awareness. Then you can fit your own personal style and taste into the general principles.

7. **Ask How You Look.**

   The simplest way to get immediate feedback is to ask others. Although people will be sensitive, if you are continuously open and forthright by asking ''how does this look'', and ''how does that look'', you will gain a valuable perspective on yourself. Don't be shy. Others will soon realize you are serious and give you their honest opinions. Once this happens your dress and appearance will become more and more effective.

PERSONAL GOAL WORKSHEET

Habits to Evaluate:

Write down three of your habitual patterns regarding your dress and appearance that you may want to modify, strengthen or lose:

1.

2.

3.

Then write what you plan to practice to modify, strengthen or change each habit.

1.

2.

3.

Remember: Practice Makes Permanent

BEHAVIORAL SKILL #5: VOICE AND VOCAL VARIETY

> *"The Devil hath not, in all his quiver's choice,*
> *An arrow for the heart like a sweet voice."*
> *Byron*

IS YOUR VOICE AN ASSET?

Checklist:
Determine the answer for each question listed below. Repeat this exercise again after you have completed this chapter. You still may need more time **experiencing** your communication relationships to check every box, but review the book on a regular basis until you can complete all of them.

YES   NO

☐ ☐ Does your voice project to others or do you simply speak?

☐ ☐ Do you know if you have a high nasal or low resonant voice, or somewhere in between?

☐ ☐ Are you aware when your voice goes into a monotone, and for what reasons?

☐ ☐ Has anyone ever complimented you on your nice voice? (If so, why? If not, why not?)

☐ ☐ Does your telephone voice differ from your speaking voice?

☐ ☐ Are you aware of what impact your voice has over the phone?

☐ ☐ Do you know how to put a "smile" in your voice?

☐ ☐ When you hear a person answer a phone for an organization do you think about what kind of image is conveyed?

☐ ☐ Do you know what impact the tone your voice has compared to the content of your message?

BEHAVIORAL OBJECTIVE

...to learn to use your voice as a rich, resonant instrument, especially when you are communicating with others in person, on the phone, or in a group setting. To command their attention and not allow your voice to be a barrier to action.

WHAT SOME PEOPLE DO

- Albert is a well-known author. He has written two block-buster, non-fiction best sellers on new trends in business. Chris, a professional speaker, was fascinated with Albert's ideas, and drove two hundred miles to hear him speak. Chris was fascinated with his ideas, but fell asleep within fifteen minutes of the opening of Albert's presentation which was a flat dull monotone. Albert's voice became a barrier to the exciting vibrancy of his ideas. Little communication occurrred.

- A world famous football player and world famous golfer shared one common distinction. They both, at the peak of their profession, were perceived as giants in highly competitive sports. Both have abnormally high pitched voices. This has always been a shock to people who have heard them speak for the first time. The reality is that their authority suffers because their voices are inconsistent with the image. They do very few speaking commercials. With their stature they could probably increase their income a million dollars per year through speaking endorsements—if they would work on their tone of voice.

- A well-known chief executive officer of a steel company gave a dedication to a new building in a major city. He read his speech in the bright outdoors to approximately a thousand people. What he did not know was that page ten of his speech was inadvertently copied twice. He read it twice. Since he was not paying attention to the words, he didn't realize he had read it twice. What was worse, the audience didn't know he had read it twice either. Only his speech writer and a smattering of others were aware of this gaff. He talked in a monotone. By the time he got to page ten, nobody was really listening, including himself.

- Sue and her twin sister were called "the squeaky twins" when they were cheerleaders in high school. Their voices were high pitched, and dramatically stood out even in the middle of a loud and exciting game. Sue began working on improving her voice using exercises similar to those listed later in this book. After just a couple of months, several people became aware of the difference in vocal resonance between Sue and her twin sister when they were together.

- A major investment company recently went public. The executives who spoke at the initial public offering meetings read their prospectus, with very little vocal energy. There was equally little excitement generated by the public offering, even though the figures they talked about were excellent.

IMPROVING YOUR VOICE AND VOCAL VARIETY

Your voice is the primary vehicle to carry your message. It is like transportation—you can have an old jalopy that rattles along or a smooth running, finely tuned automobile. Both will get you to your destination, but the quality of the ride can vary greatly.

Your Voice Transmits Energy   The excitement and the enthusiasm you feel should be directly conveyed by the sound of your voice. We quickly get in vocal habit patterns that are difficult to change. They *can* however be changed or relearned. Record your voice to become aware about *how much, or how little, energy you transmit to others.*

Your Vocal Tone and Quality Can Count for 84% of "Your Message"   Professor Mehrabian's research shows that your vocal tone; intonation, resonance and delivery accounts for 84% of the believability you have *when people can't see you.* For example, when you talk on the telephone.

The Sound of One Word   Subtleties of voice are far greater than we think. We can read an enormous amount into the vocal tone of people on the telephone during the first few seconds. Call someone you know well and listen as they say, "hello." You can almost tell what their exact mood by that single word.

The Four Aspects of Voice   The four components that make up your vocal expression are relaxation, breathing, projection and resonance. Each can be altered through exercises to expand your vocal effectiveness. All work together to give your voice their unique characteristics.

Use Vocal Variety   Vocal variety is a great way to keep people interested and involved. Use a "roller coaster" where you consciously lift your voice and then let it plummet. This will make you aware of a monotone and get you in the habit of putting variety into your voice.

Don't Read Speeches   One of the greatest culprits of a monotone delivery is in reading aloud. Writing, reading and speaking are different communication mediums. Use notes and outlines of main ideas when you speak. This will allow you to let your mind spontaneously select words. This will force your voice to be active, animated and natural because you are continuously thinking, adapting, and altering your content.

EXERCISES IN AWARENESS AND SKILL DEVELOPMENT

1. **Emphasize the Right Word.**
   Take the sentence "Now is the time for change". Read it emphasizing a different word each time. Notice the difference in the meaning, depending on which word you emphasize. Emphasis is critically important. Experiment emphasizing the appropriate word in your every day conversations.

2. **The Voice of the Company.**
   Call five companies at random from the phone book and rate them by the vocal tone and quality of the way they answer the phone. How does *your* organization rate on initial image. And how do you *personally* rate when you answer your telephone?

3. **Good and Bad Voices.**
   List five people you know with attractive, pleasant vocal deliveries. List five people you know who have poor vocal deliveries. Analyze why they are good or bad.

4. **Record Yourself.**
   The best excercise to develop your vocal skills is to record yourself. Do it as often as possible. Record a telephone conversation, record a business meeting, record a conversation with a friend, ect. Even record casual conversations using a dictaphone. *The most important improvement mechanism for your vocal delivery is getting audio feedback.*

5. **Voice Exercises.**
   For each of the following exercises, stand leaning forward in the ready position and maintain a deep, easy breathing pattern throughout.

   A. *For Improved Breathing, Breathe From the Diaphragm*
      1. Place your hands on your lower rib cage.
      2. Inhale deeply through your nose. The expansion you feel in your lower rib cage is caused by your diaphragm muscle expanding and dropping as the air pushes against it. Your shoulders should not move.
      3. Exhale, allowing the air to slowly escape through your slightly open mouth. You will feel a depression around your lower rib cage as the diaphragm rises like a trampoline to support and propel the air.
      4. Repeat steps 1-3 several times until you find your rhythm where breathing is effortless. There should be a sensation of being calm yet full of energy.
      5. Do the exercise one more time, moving one hand from the side of your lower rib cage. When you inhale, your breath should push your hand away from the abdominal area. If this does not happen, you are not breathing deeply enough for the diaphragm to do its job. *Remember*: while inhaling, the abdominal area should fill up first and more fully than your chest.

VOICE EXERCISES (Continued)

5. B. *To Improve Sounds You Make While Breathing*

    1. Repeat the instructions from the previous exercise, but when you exhale, do it on the sound of "AH".

    2. Relax your jaw, open your mouth and sustain in the "AH" for as long as it is strong and lively. (Do not let yourself run out of air and be sure not to put tension in your throat.)

C. *Learn to Tone and Relax Your Head and Neck*

    1. Relax your jaw so your mouth is slightly open.

    2. Slowly drop (don't push) your head to your chest—bring it back to the center—drop it to your right shoulder, then back to center—drop it to your left shoulder, then back to center—drop it to the back, return to center.

    3. Beginning at center, do two head rolls slowly to the right. Return to center and do two head rolls slowly to the left.

    4. Monitor your breathing throughout, make sure you are not holding your breath. Keep your jaw loose.

D. *Tone and Relax Your Shoulders*

    1. With your hands at your sides, clench your fists.

    2 Lift your shoulders to your ears (or try to!).

    3. Drop your shoulders and release your fists with a thrust, sighing as you exhale.

E. *Tone and Relax Using Shoulder Rolls*

    1. Do six slow shoulder rolls to the back, keeping your jaw loose. Feel your chest expand; sigh as you exhale.

    2. Do six slow shoulder rolls to the front. Sigh as you exhale.

F. *Tone and Relax Your Face* (also known as "the prune").

    1. Make the tiniest face you can. Pucker your lips, close your eyes and tighten your muscles.

    2. Open into the widest face you can make.

    3. Return to the tight position, then try to move your entire face to the right-hand side.

    4. Then try to move your face to the left-hand side.

    5. Return to the wide position and repeat the exercise.

VOICE EXERCISES (Continued)

5. G. *Tone and Relax Your Lips (''The Motor Boat'')*

1. Take a deep breath.
2. Pucker your lips.
3. As you exhale, force the air through your puckered lips. (This will result in a ''BRR'' sound and will direct vibrating energy to your lips while relaxing them.)

H. *Increase Your Resonance (aka ''KING KONG'' and ''YAWNING'')*

1. Drop your jaw and allow it to hang loosely.
2. Inhale deeply through your nose allowing your belly to fill up first and more fully than your chest.
   a. As you exhale, say ''KING KONG, DING DONG, BING BONG'', lowering the tone each time so that the final ''BONG'' gently eases down into a lower and lower range, until you reach bottom. Do this gently and avoid pushing on your throat muscles.
   b. As you exhale, relax your jaw. Open your mouth wide and allow your throat to open: Start on a high note, follow your pitch gradually lower until you reach bottom—as when yawning. Do this gently. Avoid pushing on your throat muscles.

I. *Learn to Project Your Voice*

1. Say a test sentence in a conversational tone.
2. Inhale deeply through your nose, allowing your belly to fill first and more fully than your chest.
3. Exhale while saying your test sentence, with the mental image of placing your voice 10-20 rows beyond the last row of an imaginary audience.
4. Monitor yourself to make sure you are letting your breath support your voice rather than pushing the sound from your throat.

J. *Control and Vary Your Pitch*

Say test sentences in a sing-song fashion. Play with different pitches and experiment with a range of tones. Song lyrics and poems work well.

K. *Practice Your Pacing*

Practice test sentences while varying the speed of your delivery between *and* within them. Insert pauses for additional variety. Tape record yourself to hear the difference. Read interesting newspaper articles aloud and exaggerate the pace.

All of the preceeding exercises need regular practice. Like learning to ride a bicycle, repeat each exercise until it becomes a habit. Whenever possible, practice with a friend.

PERSONAL GOAL WORKSHEET

Habits to Evaluate:

Write down three of your habitual patterns around your voice and vocal variety that you may want to modify, strengthen or lose:

1.

2.

3.

Then write what you plan to practice to modify, strengthen or change each habit.

1.

2.

3.

Remember: Practice Makes Permanent

BEHAVIORAL SKILL #6: LANGUAGE, PAUSES AND NON-WORDS

> *"Perhaps of all of the creations of man, language is the most astonishing."*
> *Lytton Strachey*

Do you use non-words?

Checklist:
Determine the answer for each question listed below. Repeat this exercise again after you have completed this chapter. You still may need more time **experiencing** your communication relationships to check every box, but review the book on a regular basis until you can complete all of them.

YES	NO	
[ ]	[ ]	Do you know how long you pause when you are speaking formally?
[ ]	[ ]	Does your occupation use "jargon?"
[ ]	[ ]	Do you use slang, code words or jargon in your normal conversation without realizing it?
[ ]	[ ]	Can you recall the last time you looked up a new word in the dictionary?
[ ]	[ ]	Do you know the appropriate length of a pause?
[ ]	[ ]	Do you use pauses automatically?
[ ]	[ ]	Are you able to pause for dramatic effect?
[ ]	[ ]	Do you know what the most common "non-word" is?

BEHAVIORIAL OBJECTIVE

....to use appropriate and clear language for your listeners, with planned pauses and no "non-words."

WHAT SOME PEOPLE DO

- Toni is the executive housekeeper of a major hotel chain. She is a big woman with a resonant voice and a confident air. When she talks, she ends every other sentence with "OK?". By 'asking for agreement' with an "OK?" She is inconsistent with her natural confidence and the content of her message.

- A major government official made a three minute and eleven second statement justifying an attack on an enemy position. In that short period there were 57 "umm's", er's" and "ah's". The credibility of his statement was dramatically flawed with these non-words of nervousness.

- Fred is an outstanding speech trainer. Six feet, six inches tall with a booming voice, he is good-looking, articulate and much in demand as a speaker. He also has one distraction. In conversation (as well as in speeches) he often inserts the word "sort-of" as a qualifier. This diminishes his credibility, particularly when he is making an emphatic statement. Such qualifiers are ingrained habits that are difficult to break.

IMPROVING YOUR USE OF LANGUAGE, (ADDING PAUSES AND ELIMINATING NON-WORDS)

Language is made of both words and non-words. People communicate most effectively when they are able to select the right words. This requires a rich vocabulary that can be used responsively and appropriately as the situation demands. One would not talk to a child the same way as to a group of physicists. Non-words are barriers to clear communication. Umm's, OK's, you know's, well's, and's, etc. are not only sloppy, but distracting when repeated as a habit. Pauses are an integral part of language. An effective communicator uses natural pauses between sentences. Outstanding communicators pause for dramatic effect as well.

► *Direct Language*
State and ask for what you want and mean. Dru Scott emphasizes the difference by replacing ''I'll try'' with ''I will'' or ''We can't'' with ''You can'' in her book ''CUSTOMER SATISFACTION: THE SECOND HALF OF YOUR JOB'' (see page 79 for ordering information):

''I'll try and get an answer for you''
(replace with)
''I will check and get back to you before 4 p.m.''

► *Vocabulary Increases with Use*
Children increase their vocabulary through formal study at school. Adults don't have the same motivation because we are not being directly graded. But our eduction level, clarity, and effectiveness in communications is graded daily by the choice of words we use. Anyone can increase his or her vocabulary through the active incorporation of new words.

► *Beware of Jargon*
Jargon is an excellent communication shorthand for people who share the same language. Even English words will sound like a foreign language if your listener doesn't understand your jargon.

► *The Pause—A Most Important Tool*
You can pause naturally for three to four seconds, even in the middle of a sentence. The problem is we are not used to doing it. When we do it, a three or four second pause seems like twenty seconds in our own minds. Practice *pausing and getting feedback* to learn how natural you sound when you pause. Push pausing to the limit during practice and you will do it more naturally in real conversations.

► *Replacing Non-words with Pauses*
Some people call them ''word whiskers''—those unnecessary, unwanted, (and superfluous) barriers to communication. *Don't* use umm's, ahh's, er's, and's, well's, OK's, you know's, and any other unnecessary ''pause fillers''. Record yourself and/or soliciting feedback to recognize your non-words, and then consciously concentrate to eliminate them.

EXERCISES IN AWARENESS AND SKILL DEVELOPMENT

1. *Use One New Word a Day*

   Force yourself to use one new word every day in your conversation. Find a half dozen times where you can use that word. Try words such as: dissemble, jocular, fulsome, empirical, robust, espouse, etc. The words do not have to be long or intellectual—just different. Make your own list and work at it daily.

2. *Use a Dictionary*

   Put a dictionary at your desk in your office and at home. Use it! Most of us rarely use a dictionary unless and until it becomes a habit. Just looking up each new word you read or hear will go a long way to increase your vocabulary. A larger vocabulary gives you the ability to draw on the right word or phrase, when appropriate. It does not mean you use big words to show off, simply that you are able to use the clearest, most colorful, most apt word in the right situation.

3. *Watch Your Jargon*

   We all have some jargon in our lives. List ten jargon phrases common to you. *Make yourself aware where you use them.* It's fine to use them with people who understand what they mean, but very alienating or confusing to others.

4. *Talk in Pauses*

   Talk into a tape recorder and consciously leave three second pauses. Leave those pauses between each sentence at first. Then leave a three or four second pause in the middle of a sentence. Exaggerate the pauses so they feel very long to you when you are recording them. Then on playback listen to how naturally they sound.

5. *Get Rid of Your Non-words*

   The most distracting area in language is non-words—those ''um's'' and ''ah's'' we don't need to use. There are two ways to effectively get rid of these through simple behavior modification:

   a. Ask an associate or friend to say your name every time you use your habitual non-word. For example, if you use ''umm'', every time you say ''umm'' in a conversation, ask your partner to simply state your name. They should do this without saying anything else. Your name is simply a feedback tool. Very quickly you will become sensitized to your use of that ''non-word''. Before long your mind will stop you before you say it and you will leave a pause as a replacement.

   b. Record yourself at every opportunity to sensitize yourself to your non-word. Listening to it over and over will soon remind you to leave a pause instead of the irritating, distracting non-word that you use. Record yourself on the phone, chatting or in formal situations—it does not matter. Just be sure to continue the feedback daily.

PERSONAL GOAL WORKSHEET

Habits to Evaluate:

Write down three of your habitual patterns regarding your use of language, pauses and non-words that you may want to modify, strengthen or lose:

1.

2.

3.

Then write what you plan to practice to modify, strengthen or change each habit.

1.

2.

3.

Remember: Practice Makes Permanent

BEHAVIORAL SKILL #7: LISTENER INVOLVEMENT

> *"Your listeners won't care what you say until they know that you care."*
> *Anonymous*

When your listener looks bored, do you get upset, or do you change your strategy and involve them?

Checklist:
Determine the answer for each question listed below. Repeat this exercise again after you have completed this chapter. You still may need more time **experiencing** your communication relationships to check every box, but review the book on a regular basis until you can complete all of them.

YES NO

☐ ☐ Do you know the three different forms of questions?

☐ ☐ Do you physically move around when you are in a speaking situation?

☐ ☐ Are you aware of the need to engage your audience's right brain?

☐ ☐ If you are presenting a lot of information, do you obtain regular feedback signals by involving your audience?

☐ ☐ Do you know the two most important elements of your content to involve a listener when you are talking?

BEHAVIORAL OBJECTIVE

....to maintain the active interest and involvement of each person with whom you are communicating, every time you talk—whether one person or one thousand.

WHAT SOME PEOPLE DO

* Richard is the pastor of a local church. One of his skills to keep people awake, involved, and interested during his sermons is to use humor. One morning he added something else. He held up an ''Erase-a-sketch'' toy and wrote ''SIN'' on the surface. When he described how the Lord wiped the slate clean of sin for each of us, he did the same on his prop to show a blank surface. There wasn't one person who did not get his message.

* Shirley was called in to the president's office for a meeting. She was on friendly terms with him, and waltzed into the office casually. When he got up and closed the door before saying a word, she knew the tone of this meeting was different. She was involved.

* Nick, a brilliant engineer got up at an association meeting to read a paper. And that's what he did—spent twenty minutes reading his technically oriented paper. The audience was technically oriented but only ten percent of them listened. The rest tuned Nick out within the first minute of his monotone reading.

* Stewart gave his first Toastmaster's speech, (which is called an ice-breaker). When he came to the lectern he placed on it a large object covered by a heavy cloth. Before he said a word, he took out a hammer from underneath the lectern, whipped off the covering to reveal a slab of ice and began hammering at it saying, ''This is my ice-breaker''.

IMPROVING YOUR LISTENER INVOLVEMENT SKILLS

When you speak and engage a listener with only content aimed primarily at the intellectual level, you are operating in a very narrow range. You are appealing mostly to the linear processing of the left brain. For pure information (facts and figures), this would be adequate. Realize that information can be effectively communicated in writing. People can read five times faster than you can talk.

But when you are speaking, when you are involved in interpersonal communications, you are revealing ideas and opinions. You are trying to move people to action or persuade them to agree. If you miss involving your listeners' right brain, you are missing much of your potential for impact. Listeners, whether one person in a conversation or a thousand people in an audience, are bombarded by stimuli every instant. You need to engage all of their senses and all of their mind. The more *involved* a listener is, the more you can convince and persuade that person of your message.

"SWIRLS"

A "swirl" is an 'instant' of total involvement on the mind of a listener. A swirl can be; a laugh, a mental "ah-hah!", being asked up to do an exercise, having to think of a question, deciding whether or not to volunteer, and so forth. Many "swirls" are created through humor and humanization, but they can come from any of nine listener involving techniques described below. It could be as small a thing as moving into an audience or using a different type of visual aid. A swirl is a moment of involved interest in the mind of your listener.

THE NINE LISTENER INVOLVING TECHNIQUES

There are a basic nine listener involving techniques. These can be adapted to large groups or to individual communication. They center around three areas:

1. YOUR STYLE
2. YOUR INTERACTION WITH THE LISTENER(S)
3. THE ACTUAL CONTENT OF WHAT YOU SAY

Adapt the following list during *all* of your communications, and you will continuously involve your listener *without fail*.

NINE LISTENER INVOLVING TECHNIQUES

A. STYLE

1. DRAMA

* *Create a strong opening* by announcing a serious problem, telling a moving story, or asking a rhetorical question to get each person thinking. You can also make a startling statement.

* *Include a dramatic element* such as a long pause to emphasize a key statement, vocal tone and pitch changes, or higher-intensity emotions such as anger, joy, sadness or excitement.

* *Add visual and kinesthetic detail* such as color, smell, temperature and other sensations to vividly recreate a story or experience for your listener(s).

* *End your communication* with a dramatic or inspirational quote, or firm call to action.

2. EYE COMMUNICATION

* *Survey all of your listeners* when you start speaking before beginning extended eye communication with any individual.

* *Keep your listeners involved* and engaged by maintaining 3-6 second contact with as many as possible. Don't forget ''orphans'' at the far edges of a room or along your side of a conference table during meetings.

* *Gauge the reaction of your listeners* throughout your presentation. Do they agree? Are they bored? Do they have questions?

3. MOVEMENT

* *Change the dynamics* of your presentation with *purposeful* movement. Whenever possible, move around.

* *Never back away* from your listener(s). Move towards them—especially at the beginning and the end of your communication.

NINE LISTENER INVOLVING TECHNIQUES (Continued)

4. VISUALS

* *Add variety* by using visuals. Give your listener(s) something to look at in addition to you.
* *Use different types of visual aids* in a formal presentation—for instance, use overheads *and* flip charts. Rehearse in advance so the transitions are smooth and non-distracting.
* *Get on-the-spot-listener participation by experimenting* with techniques such as writing listener concerns on a flip chart or filling in an overhead transparency as you go.

B. INTERACTION

5. QUESTIONS

There are three types of questions you can use in a group setting. Each allows you to obtain a deeper level of involvement:

* *Rhetorical questions* will keep your listeners active and thinking. This is especially valuable when you don't have time or it's not appropriate to actually discuss an issue.
* *Ask for a show of hands* to get listeners more involved and to give you a quick way to gauge their reactions.
* *Ask for a volunteer.* Even though only one person will speak or act, you can feel the adrenalin rush through the others as they consider whether they might be the volunteer.

6. DEMONSTRATIONS

* *Plan ahead for every step or procedure* and be sure to accurately time the demonstration before you use it.
* *Have a volunteer* from the group to help you in your demonstration.

7. SAMPLES/GIMMICKS

* *Have fun with your listeners.* Get them involved, but you should always stay in control of the session. Keep things appropriate for your profession as well as for your listeners.
* *If you are promoting a product,* consider using samples of it to "reward" volunteer participants.
* *Use creativity.* Gimmicks can be used effectively in most business settings. But keep things in good taste.

NINE LISTENER INVOLVING TECHNIQUES
(Continued)

C. CONTENT

8. INTEREST

* *Before you speak,* review what you plan to say by asking "How will I benefit my listeners?"

* *Remember short attention spans.* Use eye contact to gauge interest. Use examples, drama, humor, visuals and movement to engage your listener.

* *Maintain a high level of personal interest.* If you make the same presentation repeatedly, consider changing examples, getting listeners involved in different places, or changing the order of your presentation to maintain your enthusiasm.

9. HUMOR

* *Begin with a friendly, warm comment.* A personal remark will start the ball rolling and relax things.

* *Make your humor appropriate* to your listeners and relevant to your Point Of View. Be professional while allowing your "humanness" to appear.

* *Develop a sense of humor* and use it. You might tell stories, refer to current events, include one-liners, poke fun at yourself or even play off of listeners' comments.

* *If you "lay an egg",* stand back and admire it! Be willing to laugh at yourself.

EXERCISES IN AWARENESS AND SKILL DEVELOPMENT

▶ *Exercise #1 Learn From the TV Masters.*
Look at the TV talk show hosts and notice how they continuously involve their listeners and their guests. They move around, ask questions, engage individuals with eye communication, use gimmicks and props, visuals, humor, etc. Professionals use the same skills presented in this book.

▶ *Exercise #2 Use the Conversational Gambit—Answer a Question with a Question.*
A spontaneity exercise called the "hot potato" can be effective. This is where you answer a question with another question. Although it is an exercise in spontaneity as well as a sales technique for "discovery", the same exercise can be used to involve any listener in any setting. First focus on what you want to know about the person with whom you are talking, and then ask them a question about that subject. Most people will just answer and stop. Use their answer to trigger another question, geared towards the subject area of interest that you want to pursue. Often this will get the other person engaged in also asking you questions which leads to a very involved interaction. Respond to any question asked, but while you are talking, think of the *next* question that you want to ask. Your mind can think at the same time you are talking, and you can move a conversation wherever you want to go.

The "hot potato" can be practiced anywhere. It is very effective to use at dinner parties and other formal settings. A memorable Dale Carnegie story is when he sat next to a wealthy matron at a dinner party and spent the entire night asking her questions about her life. At the end of the evening she said, "What an interesting conversationalist you are, Mr. Carnegie". He had never talked about himself at all.

▶ *Exercise #3 Do It Daily.*
Take each of the nine listener involving techniques and apply one each day in your business life. When you finish the cycle of nine, start again so every day you are consciously aware of making an effort to involve people. It won't be long before it becomes a positive habit.

PERSONAL GOAL WORKSHEET

Habits to Evaluate:

Write down three of your habitual patterns regarding your listener involvement skills that you may want to modify, strengthen or lose:

1.

2.

3.

Then write what you plan to practice to modify, strengthen or change each habit.

1.

2.

3.

| **Remember:** Practice Makes Permanent |

BEHAVIORAL SKILL #8: USING HUMOR

> *"The man who causes them to laugh gets more votes for the measure than the man who forces them to think."*
>
> *Malcolm de Chazall*

Do you use humor in your communications?

Checklist:
Determine the answer for each question listed below. Repeat this exercise again after you have completed this chapter. You still may need more time **experiencing** your communication relationships to check every box, but review the book on a regular basis until you can complete all of them.

YES NO

☐ ☐ Are you funny? Do you laugh at yourself?

☐ ☐ Do you know the estimated percentage of people who know how to tell jokes well?

☐ ☐ Do you tell more than two jokes a week?

☐ ☐ Do people tend to laugh when they are around you?

☐ ☐ Do you know what makes you laugh?

BEHAVIORAL OBJECTIVE

....to create a bond between yourself and your listeners by using humor to enable them to enjoy listening to you more. To use humor as a conscious tool to make yourself more human, and to make others have a good time when they are around you.

WHAT SOME PEOPLE DO

* Beverly is the founder of a large retail outlet. She is a well known figure in the retail industry. She is also a wife and mother of two children. She was once asked at a news conference whether she would serve as a director on other company's board. Her reply was: "I don't do boards or windows."

* John is now a professional speaker who used to be a successful soccer coach. When he just missed taking his team to the national championships, the owner fired him. Shortly after that John was introduced to give a speech with a flowery introduction that forgot to mention what everybody already knew. His opening was: "You know I used to be the coach of the Kings but I got fired. I was fired because of illness and fatigue. The fans were sick and tired of me."

* Sunny has a mother in a nursing home whom she calls daily. One of her goals is to do something to make her mother laugh in every phone call. She always is able to succeed.

* The most memorable event in the 1984 U.S. presidential debates was Ronald Reagan's humorous response to the question of age. He said that he would not make a campaign issue of Walter Mondale being too young. In almost all of the presidential debates, the most vivid memories are usually from comments that have been made in humor or jest.

IMPROVING YOUR USE OF HUMOR

Humor is one of the most important skills for effective interpersonal communication, yet one of the most elusive. Some people are naturally personable and likable. Others have to work at. Humor is a learnable skill and we can all learn to use this important tool more effectively.

► *Don't Tell Jokes*
Approximately one in every one hundred persons is a good teller of jokes, but ten times that number *think* they can tell jokes well. Unless you really are effective at pacing, delivery and style, don't try telling jokes in formal situations.

► *Do Tell Stories and Anecdotes*
We are funny, humorous and human when we open ourselves to be vulnerable—to be part of the human comedy. There is much to be gained in interpersonal communications in telling humorous asides, stories, anecdotes, or reactions.

► *Humanization Is Humor*
In most interpersonal communications, comedy is not really what we are after. Rather, we want to connect on the personal level with our listeners. That connection is most often made on a level of ''likeability''. This quality comes through factors such as being: personal, open, friendly, caring, interested, personable, emotional, concerned, pleasant, comfortable, confident, unselfish, feeling and fun.

► *Remember ''The Personality Factor''*
We previously learned that people often vote for political leaders on the basis of likeability. Others ''vote'' on whether they agree with you or support your position on the basis of ''The Personality Factor.'' This factor is most characterized by the level of humor or humanization that you project.

► *Your Smile Is What People See*
When we are talking, people look at our face. The predominant feature is our smile. This important feature of our physiognomy shows quickly whether we are excited, enthused, angry, serious or somewhere in between. Our sense of humor is largely perceived non-verbally through a smile. It is important to know your natural ''smileability.''

► *People Learn Best Through Humor*
Some of the most effective swirls come from moments of lightness or involvement. Those emotional moments are the best time to get your message through. You reach both the right brain and the left brain when you use humor and humanization.

EXERCISES IN AWARENESS AND SKILL DEVELOPMENT

1. *Determine What Makes You Laugh*
   Find out more about your sense of humor. Do you have a dry wit, or like earthy stories? Do you have an infectious laugh, or exhibit an easy smile? Everybody is different, yet most of us love to laugh and have fun. Find out what your "humor profile" is. Ask others to rate your sense of humor on a scale of one to ten.

2. *Make Someone Laugh*
   People can consciously use humor. In a few seconds, one person can make another person (or a group of people) laugh, smile, chuckle, chortle, or relax— *if they work at it.* By putting humor as a conscious goal, everything that passes through one's mind will automatically look for the connection that relates to the human comedy.

3. *Think Funny*
   Although this is sometimes difficult to do, it is also one of the most helpful. People who laugh easily tend to filter their world through a screen of humor. They look for the bright side rather than the dark side. They can turn a crisis into an opportunity. Think "funny" on a conscious level. Take your subject seriously but don't take yourself seriously. You will be surprised at how this conscious effort will enable you to be more spontaneous, open and fun.

4. *Gain Awareness Through Feedback*
   Record yourself on audio tape at every formal presentation you give. Make a conscious effort to use humor and see how it works in the feedback. Count the laughs, chuckles, smiles that you are able to generate from your audience.

5. *Watch Others*
   We all know people we enjoy being around. We want to be with them because they are fun, light and lively. Search these people out. Observe to see how they involve others. These are not people who are usually comics or jokesters, but individuals who continuously create "swirls" in their interpersonal communications. Experiment with trying some of their habits, and adapting them to your style.

6. *Keep a Humor Journal*
   In your journal or diary, keep a page for quotes, quips, anecdotes, stories and "funny things" that happen in your daily life. Consciously keep it for a week, marking down ten "light" items in your life each day. If you don't have ten, work harder at humor. Life is meant to be joyful.

PERSONAL GOAL WORKSHEET

Habits to Evaluate:

Write down three of your habitual patterns regarding your use of humor that you may want to modify, strengthen or lose:

1.

2.

3.

Then write what you plan to practice to modify, strengthen or change each habit.

1.

2.

3.

Remember: Practice Makes Permanent

BEHAVIORAL SKILL #9: THE NATURAL SELF

"When we encounter a natural style we are always surprised and delighted, for we thought to see an author, and found a man."

Pascal

Who are you in other's eyes?

Checklist:
Determine the answer for each question listed below. Repeat this exercise again after you have completed this chapter. You still may need more time **experiencing** your communication relationships to check every box, but review the book on a regular basis until you can complete all of them.

YES NO

☐ ☐ Are you more comfortable speaking to a small group of people, in front of a large audience, in a high pressure one-on-one sales situation . . . or none of the above?

☐ ☐ Do you know in which of the four stages of speaking you normally reside?

☐ ☐ Do you know what behavioral changes you experience during high stress communications?

☐ ☐ Do you know your three strongest communication skill areas?

☐ ☐ What about your three weakest communication areas?

☐ ☐ Can you list your strengths and weaknesses?

BEHAVIORAL OBJECTIVE

....to be authentic. To be yourself in all communication circumstances, understanding and using your natural strengths, and building communication weaknesses into strengths. To have the confidence in your mental spontaneity to adapt to the circumstance.

WHAT SOME PEOPLE DO

* In an isolated area of Italy, there is a small town surrounded by mountains with craggy cliffs and caves. People moved into these caves and over time were looked on with disdain by the town dwellers.

The hermit "cave colony" did no harm. They lived by themselves in isolated and primitive circumstances. One year, a cruel young man named Simon began work at the town foundry. He organized a gang that regularly harassed the cave people. After a few years of abuse, something unusual happened.

On a quiet Sunday morning, a cave dweller named Rolando came down from the hills. He calmly walked to the town square and began speaking. He was dressed in scraggly clothes. He did not have formal schooling, or social grace. But he talked with confident conviction. A crowd gathered. He asked why the peaceful cave dwellers were being persecuted. He described their lives in the cave, and the unhappiness that was caused by Simon and his gang.

Although Rolando had a simple vocabulary, he held the crowd enthralled with his message. He spoke confidently, as he spoke from his heart. He was a natural. From that day forward, harassing of the cave dwellers stopped.

IMPROVING YOUR NATURAL SELF

Think of the most forceful speaker you know. Think of the most impressive leader you know.

In each case, you will not find one who is a copy of anybody else. We each are different. Each with our own strengths and weaknesses. Although this is a simple concept, it gains complexity when you consider the thousands of variables in our interpersonal communications. We have resources to draw on—natural strengths that are already there, as well as areas to make into strengths.

The previous behavioral skill areas presented in this book are essential if you expect to become an effective communicator:

The Natural Self

Being your natural self is as much a skill as the eight you have read about. Although an attitude, it is what you can do with that attitude to:

1. Acknowledge your strengths and your weak areas, and
2. Convert your weaknesses into strengths

From the eight previous behavioral skills (see list on page 77 if you cannot recall them), list in order the three that reflect your greatest strengths:

1. _____
2. _____
3. _____

Now list the three that are weaknesses for you, with the weakest first:

1. _____
2. _____
3. _____

IMPROVING YOUR NATURAL SELF
(Continued)

► *Learn Like a Juggler*
If you ever learned to juggle, you probably learned to start with one ball first just to get the rhythm, then add another to practice with both hands working together. Finally, you practiced adding a third ball until you could juggle.

Becoming an expert in interpersonal communications is much like juggling. You master one skill at a time, and add to them once they become a habit.

First, acknowledge your natural strengths and be thankful you don't have to learn them from scratch. Realize that many others do. You may have an easy, natural smile, where others may have to work at lightening themselves up in their interpersonal communications. On the other hand, you may find it difficult to gesture naturally, where another might have been born more effusive. Acknowledge those strengths and work to improve and capitalize on them. Next, work on the weaknesses, one at a time, until they become strengths. Take your weakest area first and concentrate on improving it every day for a week. Eye communication may be a difficult skill for you to master. Put your conscious mental energy into developing extended eye communication each day for a week or two. Then move to another skill. Continue that process until you have gone through all nine skills.

► *Communicating Well Is a Lifetime Process*
No one is a completed, effective communicator. We always find new unwanted habits that pop up, as well old undesirable habits that creep back. We also find new strengths that occur as we mature and as we experiment with various behavioral skills. Often synergy occurs where a new-found habit will work to improve an old habit. Or two habits work together to form an effective new behavior. For example, movement and extended eye communication can breed confidence that allows somebody to maintain excellent eye communication with an individual and even allow perhaps a reaching out and touching the arm of the listener.

Finally, remember that interpersonal communication is a multitude of skills. Also remember that skills can be learned and practiced. It is our hope that you are on your way to mastering the *ART OF COMMUNICATING.*

Good Luck!

EXERCISES IN AWARENESS AND SKILL DEVELOPMENT

1. Show the list of the nine behavioral skills (page 77) to five different people, and ask each person to rank you from your greatest strength to your greatest weakness. Observe what others see in you. Compare the responses and match your self-perceptions. If they match, you know where to start work. If they don't, take those areas that are least consistent and work on them first.

2. Use the following feedback sheet and ask three people to fill one out in detail following your next presentation. Again, match the consistency with those previously established in the nine behavioral skill areas. Also note any change and improvement you have as the result of feedback.

COACHING FEEDBACK SHEET

Overall Impression	Excellent	Good	Needs Work	Comments
Appearance	_____	_____	_____	_____
Enthusiasm	_____	_____	_____	_____
Posture	_____	_____	_____	_____
Expression	_____	_____	_____	_____
Content				
Opening	_____	_____	_____	_____
Listener Involvement	_____	_____	_____	_____
Word Pictures	_____	_____	_____	_____
Examples/Quotes	_____	_____	_____	_____
No Jargon	_____	_____	_____	_____
Closing	_____	_____	_____	_____
Delivery and Skills				
Extended Eye Contact	_____	_____	_____	_____
Natural Gestures	_____	_____	_____	_____
Non-word Usage	_____	_____	_____	_____
Pauses	_____	_____	_____	_____
Voice	_____	_____	_____	_____
Natural Movement	_____	_____	_____	_____
Humor	_____	_____	_____	_____
Visual Aids	_____	_____	_____	_____

(This form may be copied without further permission)

PERSONAL GOAL WORKSHEET

Habits to Evaluate:

Write down three of your habitual patterns regarding your natural self that you may want to modify, strengthen or lose:

1.

2.

3.

Then write what you plan to practice to modify, strengthen or change each habit.

1.

2.

3.

Remember: Practice Makes Permanent

SECTION III

The Nine Behavioral Skills To Effective Interpersonal Communication

SKILL

1. **Solid Eye Communication...**"to learn to look sincerely and steadily at another person."

2. **Good Posture...**"to learn to stand tall and move naturally and easily."

3. **Natural Gestures...**"to learn to be relaxed and natural when you speak."

4. **Appropriate Dress and Appearance...**"to dress, groom and appear appropriate for the environment you are in."

5. **Voice and Vocal Variety...**"to learn to use your voice as a rich, resonant instrument."

6. **Effective Use of Language and Pauses...**"to use appropriate and clear language with planned pauses and no non-words."

7. **Active Listener Involvement...**"to maintain the active interest and involvement of each person with whom you are communicating."

8. **Effective Use of Humor...**"to use humor to create a bond between yourself and your listener."

9. **Being Your Natural Self...**"to be authentic."

NOTES

FOR OTHER FIFTY-MINUTE SELF-STUDY BOOKS
SEE THE BACK OF THIS BOOK.

ABOUT THE FIFTY-MINUTE SERIES

We hope you enjoyed this book and found it valuable. If so, we have good news for you. This title is part of the best selling *FIFTY-MINUTE Series* of books. All other books are similar in size and identical in price. Several books are supported with a training video. These are identified by the symbol **Ⓥ** next to the title.

Since the first *FIFTY-MINUTE* book appeared in 1986, more than five million copies have been sold worldwide. Each book was developed with the reader in mind. The result is a concise, high quality module written in a positive, readable self-study format.

FIFTY-MINUTE Books and Videos are available from your distributor or from Crisp Publications, Inc., 95 First Street, Los Altos, CA 94022. A free current catalog is available on request.

The complete list of *FIFTY-MINUTE Series* Books and Videos are listed on the following pages and organized by general subject area.

MANAGEMENT TRAINING (Cont.)

PERSONNEL/HUMAN RESOURCES

COMMUNICATIONS

CUSTOMER SERVICE/SALES TRAINING (CONT.)

SMALL BUSINESS/FINANCIAL PLANNING

ADULT LITERACY/BASIC LEARNING

CAREER BUILDING

To order books/videos from the FIFTY-MINUTE Series, please:

1. **CONTACT YOUR DISTRIBUTOR**
   or
2. **Write to Crisp Publications, Inc.**
   95 First Street   **(415) 949-4888 - phone**
   Los Altos, CA 94022   **(415) 949-1610 - FAX**